DATE DUE   SEP 0 5

GAYLORD			PRINTED IN U.S.A.

SandCastle 3

Homographs

Bass Cannot Play Bass

Carey Molter

ABDO
Publishing Company

JACKSON COUNTY LIBRARY SERVICES
MEDFORD, OREGON 97501

Published by SandCastle™, an imprint of ABDO Publishing Company, 4940 Viking Drive, Edina, Minnesota 55435.
Cover and interior photo credits: Digital Vision, Eyewire Images, PhotoDisc,
    Rubberball Productions, Stockbyte

Library of Congress Cataloging-in-Publication Data

Molter, Carey, 1973-
    Bass cannot play bass / Carey Molter.
        p. cm. -- (Homographs)
    Includes index.
    Summary: Photographs and simple text introduce homophones, words with different meanings that are spelled the same but sound different.
    ISBN 1-57765-793-4
    1. English language--Homonyms--Juvenile literature. [1. English language--Homonyms.] I. Title.

PE1595 .M65 2002
428.1--dc21

                                                            2001053317

The SandCastle concept, content, and reading method have been reviewed and approved by a national advisory board including literacy specialists, librarians, elementary school teachers, early childhood education professionals, and parents.

Let Us Know

After reading the book, SandCastle would like you to tell us your stories about reading. What is your favorite page? Was there something hard that you needed help with? Share the ups and downs of learning to read. We want to hear from you! To get posted on the ABDO Publishing Company Web site, send us email at:

sandcastle@abdopub.com

About SandCastle™

Nonfiction books for the beginning reader

- Basic concepts of phonics are incorporated with integrated language methods of reading instruction. Most words are short, and phrases, letter sounds, and word sounds are repeated.

- Book levels are based on the ATOS™ for Books formula. Other considerations for readability include the number of words in each sentence, the number of characters in each word, and word lists based on curriculum frameworks.

- Full-color photography reinforces word meanings and concepts.

- "Words I Can Read" list at the end of each book teaches basic elements of grammar, helps the reader recognize the words in the text, and builds vocabulary.

- Reading levels are indicated by the number of flags on the castle.

SandCastle uses the following definitions for this series:

- Homographs: words that are spelled the same but sound different and have different meanings. *Easy memory tip: "-graph"= same look*

- Homonyms: words that are spelled and sound the same but have different meanings. *Easy memory tip: "-nym"= same name*

- Homophones: words that sound alike but are spelled differently and have different meanings. *Easy memory tip: "-phone"= sound alike*

Look for more SandCastle books in these three reading levels:

Level 1 (one flag)	**Level 2** (two flags)	**Level 3** (three flags)

Grades Pre-K to K 5 or fewer words per page	**Grades K to 1** 5 to 10 words per page	**Grades 1 to 2** 10 to 15 words per page

Note: Many of the pages in this book have fewer than 10 words due to the difficulty of the subject matter.

Homographs are words that are spelled the same but sound different and have different meanings.

Ben plays bass for fun.

The bass is a type of fish.

Lisa and her mom ride bikes.

Lisa is in the lead.

My new pencils have many colors of lead.

Jane goes to horse shows.

She is a shower of horses.

Mimi enjoys the cool shower
from the sprinkler.

The nurse put a bandage on his wound.

Kale is excited.

He is wound up.

My grandma is a great sewer.

She made me this hat!

The **sewer** is underground.

Our new **house** has a nice front yard.

We house this cat.

It lives inside with us.

Faye has her thumb in her
mouth.

Sam likes to **mouth** the words when he reads.

He does not read out loud.

The front of a boat is called the bow.

My sister gave me a present.

What is it topped with?

(bow)

Words I Can Read

Nouns

A noun is a person, place, or thing

bandage (BAN-dij) p. 12

bass (BASS) p. 7

bass (BAYSS) p. 6

bikes (BIKESS) p. 8

boat (BOTE) p. 20

bow (BOH) p. 21

bow (BOU) p. 20

cat (KAT) p. 17

colors (KUHL-urz) p. 9

fish (FISH) p. 7

front (FRUHNT) p. 20

fun (FUHN) p. 6

grandma (GRAND-mah) p. 14

hat (HAT) p. 14

homographs (HOM-uh-grafss) p. 5

horse shows (HORSS SHOHZ) p. 10

horses (HORSS-ez) p. 10

house (HOUSS) p. 16

lead (LED) p. 9

lead (LEED) p. 8

meanings (MEE-ningz) p. 5

mom (MOM) p. 8

mouth (MOUTH) p. 18

nurse (NURSS) p. 12

pencils (PEN-suhlz) p. 9

present (PREZ-uhnt) p. 21

sewer (SOH-ur) p. 14

sewer (SOO-ur) p. 15

shower (SHOH-ur) p. 10

shower (SHOU-ur) p. 11

sister (SISS-tur) p. 21

sprinkler (SPRINGK-lur) p. 11

thumb (THUHM) p. 18

type (TIPE) p. 7

words (WURDZ) pp. 5, 19

wound (WOOND) p. 12

yard (YARD) p. 16

Proper Nouns

A proper noun is the name of a person, place, or thing

Ben (BEN) p. 6

Faye (FAY) p. 18

Jane (JAYN) p. 10

Kale (KAYL) p. 13

Lisa (LEE-suh) p. 8

Mimi (MEE-mee) p. 11

Sam (SAM) p. 19

Pronouns

A pronoun is a word that replaces a noun

he (HEE) pp. 13, 19   she (SHEE) pp. 10, 14   we (WEE) p. 17

it (IT) pp. 17, 21   us (UHSS) p. 17   what (WUHT) p. 21

me (MEE) pp. 14, 21

Verbs

A verb is an action or being word

are (AR) p. 5   house (HOUZ) p. 17   put (PUT) p. 12

called (KAWLD) p. 20   is (IZ) pp. 7, 8, 10, 13, 14,   read (REED) p. 19

does (DUHZ) p. 19   15, 20, 21   reads (REEDZ) p. 19

enjoys (en-JOIZ) p. 11   likes (LIKESS) p. 19   ride (RIDE) p. 8

gave (GAYV) p. 21   lives (LIVZ) p. 17   sound (SOUND) p. 5

goes (GOHZ) p. 10   made (MAYD) p. 14   spelled (SPELD) p. 5

has (HAZ) pp. 16, 18   mouth (mouTH) p. 19   topped (TOPT) p. 21

have (HAV) pp. 5, 9   plays (PLAYZ) p. 6   wound (WOUND) p. 13

Adjectives

An adjective describes something

cool (KOOL) p. 11   front (FRUHNT) p. 16   my (MYE) pp. 9, 14, 21

different (DIF-ur-uhnt)   great (GRAYT) p. 14   new (NOO) pp. 9, 16

    p. 5   her (HUR) pp. 8, 18   nice (NISSE) p. 16

excited (ek-SITE-ed)   his (HIZ) p. 12   our (OUR) p. 16

    p. 13   many (MEN-ee) p. 9   this (THISS) pp. 14, 17

Adverbs

An adverb tells how, when, or where something happens

out loud (OUT LOUD) p. 19

same (SAYM) p. 5

underground (UHN-dur-ground) p. 15

up (UHP) p. 13

24